THE ADULTERY POEMS

OTHER BOOKS
BY NANCY HOLMES

Valancy and the New World
Kalamalka Press, 1988

Down to the Golden Chersonese: Victorian Lady Travellers
Sono Nis, 1991

The
Adultery
Poems

Nancy Holmes

RONSDALE PRESS

THE ADULTERY POEMS
Copyright © 2002 Nancy Holmes

RONSDALE PRESS
3350 West 21st Avenue
Vancouver, B.C., Canada
V6S 1G7

Set in New Baskerville: 11 pt on 13.5
Typesetting: Julie Cochrane
Printing: AGMV Marquis, Québec
Cover Art: Teresa Posyniak, *First Scene* (1998), 44" x 36",
    mixed media on paper
Cover Design: Julie Cochrane
Back Cover Author Photo: Linda L'abbé

Ronsdale Press wishes to thank the Canada Council for the Arts, the Government of Canada through the Book Publishing Industry Development Program (BPIDP), and the Province of British Columbia through the British Columbia Arts Council for their support of its publishing program.

NATIONAL LIBRARY OF CANADA CATALOGUING IN PUBLICATION

Holmes, Nancy, 1959–
    The adultery poems

    Poems.
    ISBN 0-921870-98-1

    I. Title.
PS8565.O637A88 2002   C811'.54   C2002-910649-4
PR9199.3.H58155A88 2002

CONTENTS

ACKNOWLEDGEMENTS

Some of these poems, or versions of them, have been published in *The Road Home, Event, The Gaspereau Review, The Fiddlehead, Orbis (U.K.), Kairos, The New Quarterly, The Malahat Review, Matrix, Textual Studies in Canada, The Antigonish Review, The Harpweaver, A Room of One's Own, Pottersfield Portfolio,* and *Other Voices.*

I'd like to thank the BC Ministry of Culture, Tourism and Small Business for a grant which enabled me to complete this manuscript. Thanks to Tom Wayman, P.K. Page, Christopher Wiseman and Karen Connelly for their support. Thanks to Harold Rhenisch and Ronald Hatch for editing and advice.

The quotations from Ovid are from the following edition:
Ovid: The Erotic Poems. Trans. Peter Green. London:
Penguin Books, 1982.

Our sport is ended: high time to quit this creative venture,
  Turn loose the swans that drew my poet's car.
As once the young men, so now let my girl-disciples
  Inscribe their trophies: "Ovid was my guide."

— Ovid, *The Art of Love*, Book III, 809-812

PART I

—

THE ART AND CRAFT
OF CAPITULATION

. . . Such joys attend you in your thirties:
Nature does not bestow them on green youth.
— Ovid, *The Art of Love,* Book II, 693-694

Picking Tulips

All April afternoon,
spring tries to be enticing —
its long warm arms,
the indelicate assault of the birds,
the lubricating rain —

but my thoughts keep turning to winter.

When out of nowhere
a jell-o mob of joy jumps forward,
loops around my ankles,
boings my eyeballs,
somersaults across my guilt.

"Sing!" they knock their red and yellow bells.
"Look!" they wink their charcoal lashes.

I am caught, surrounded, reeled,
throttled, jigged and shaken till I drop.
Thrown down in the dirt among the clowns!

It's desperate measures now.
I crawl on my hands and knees,
beat off their circus tricks,
reach right into their leafy jaws

and — slash.

Rejoice and warble now you sinners,
now that I've slit your gorgeous throats.

The Wrong Frame of Mind

Canada is not the land for the idle sensualist.
                                    — Catharine Parr Traill

Oh god, let us not be idle
look at Alberta, look at her —
her bare body rolls down sated
after the orgy of mountains
but does she stop then?
No.
Her skin springs into wheat and grass
and luscious hair
wild to be combed and scratched
with the pelts and feet of wandering animals
and the giant rake of the machine
that slides and delves.
An ecstasy of liquid willow
rubs in every fold and crevice
and in the huge bald tongue of the sky
the hawk's wing is but
a grain of salt licked off her heaving back.
Oh yes
look at the doe's wet eye
the hairy crack of crocus
the flagellant storm
the veined leg of the elk
the warm bark of the tree
that strips before the saw
and Catharine, Catharine
tell me that
again.

When We Hadn't Kissed Yet

to what does a kiss refer
and what meets most —
the lips or the skin?

refer to the mouth
and it refers back

show your hand
and we have the pale fret of the wrist

the warm blade that ploughs
the skin of the back
reminds us
of the hollow behind the knee
and another place for knives

oh turn over
and move on up

it takes two minds
to lift the page

so turn back now
or shut up

the eye can only read one way

What Do I Want?

*Though Australia may offer the temptation of greater
wages to female servants . . . rather bring them to
Canada than form connexions with such characters as
swarm the streets of Melbourne or Geelong.*
                                                    — Catharine Parr Traill

Do I really want those everyday men?
The fine upstanding men of Canada?
The woodsman who hacks the forest off the mountain?
The cowboy who straps his guns and leather to the back of his
    pretty mare?
The *coureur de bois* who aims his fragile canoe down a bruising
    sluice of thunder?

It's the sweat *they* love,
the salty foam that makes them shine and smile.
The surface is all.
They do the male dance, just once,
and then they're tested.
For the rest of their lives,
they brag about the cheap whores of Spain
and the drunken brawls in the North.

Come on,
let's emigrate with dreams, girls.
We don't need mounties or lumberjacks,
or guys with skidoos on the backs of their trucks.

Let's look for the rogues, the rakes,
the heart stoppers:
the pale musicians in the Melbourne suburbs,
the Byronic accountants of Geelong.

Whoops, A Speeding Ticket

Today I learned make love, not poems,
for poems are far too true.
You gleefully write about driving too fast:
next day the cops get you.

Whereas chances are if you make love,
your lover won't remember
the difference between the fuck in May
and the first one in December.

Latin for "Ditch"

is vulva.
Funny how this makes me think
of that ad I saw for the new female condom.
It's called "Reality."
My brain does a back flip.
Why do men get condoms called
"Ramses," "Sheik," "Supreme"?
And we get a dose of reality again?
What about "Tunnel of Love"?
Wasn't that good enough?
What about "Vortex"?
Too flippant? Having too much fun?
Or "Lovers' Lane" or "Whirlpool"?
Reality my ass.

The bastards.

And come to think of it,
he really ditched me good.

No Longer An Even Keel:
The Voyage Begins

i.

the keel is bone
the sail is skin
the ship moves in blood

and a storm stalks the body

the captain broods in the teak cabin
mutinies   lights
a fire on each submerged
and rum-soaked timber

orders a freak course

wants the red stab of coral

the relief

ii.

the keel is your wallet in my room
my mind in your files
your hand in my stockings
my bad dream in your sleep

the keel is empty glasses and oyster shells
in the afternoon

the keel lies
moves and lies
moves on
wet and pearled with lies
down deep

iii.

see, I said,
wanting to go overboard,

look at the liquid ditch
that it makes

iv.

I have a bad keel; I can't keep it down.
All night I ache from wrestling it into the water.
It wants to be the part that flies in the wind,
not the part that's loaded with lake.
The keel loves vivid scenery, and hates to live in a blur.
It belongs in the embrace of the weeds,
but it wants to show them the light.
The keel dreams of going soft and being rolled up tight.

So what can I do? Drown it? Beach it?
Let it crack and bake on some bone-dry rack?

Maybe that's just the thing. Some old-fashioned exposure.
A sizzling confession, some blistering shame.

v.

The storm drags the sail kicking and screaming
into its belly.
The keel zippers the lake's cold bag.

My hand takes leave of the rope
for a draught of salt water.

The rope that held the zigzag course

has been let go.

Let go of me.

Let go.

A New Year's Day Ending

January's frozen in unfolding,
new snow unpressed by air. Trees in glass
preserve the fruit for amber beaks of waxwings,
tangy icy berries of the mountain ash.

Our warm bodies beneath the snowy sheets
lie bare and battered, a stretch of hill
and root and bone.

We feel winter in each other. The tree's
an old tree, the buried branches uphold
the secrets of our bodies.

We never tell how other lovers touched us;
but each New Year will smother that old richness.

PART II

–

THE DITCH

The Love Triangle

They are a Valentine heart.
Their bodies have swollen into huge ventricles
that bump against each other.

Between them is the plunging point.
There, at the bottom, the poem is pinched into a corner.
The poem belongs to the love triangle.
It is the point of love.

Of course, the woman knows about the poem
but she keeps it secret.
She goes out to a payphone on the street
so they can talk.

But the poem is getting restless,
needy.
It is tired of sneaking around.
What's the point?
it says.

They argue for hours.
She pleads with it,
but to no avail.

The poem is ready to give it all
away.

The Pronouncement

she is the adulteress
he is the lover
I am the poem

I watch their love double, triple on the vine
the sun bludgeons every blossom into fruit
until all at once they are too many
hearts huffing and puffing in the heat
ripe tomatoes
limbs staked and bound
but fingers fumble with the wire

animals begin to ransack the sunny cages
take mouthfuls of flesh
eat every bit of dripping meat
the juice, the pulp,
even the thin glove of skin
and the seeds in their amber jelly

winter comes
he is stripped and harvested
she is scrapped and tossed away

while I am the animal, the cage
and I bide my time
wait for more

The Adulteress in a Ditch

A dirty book,
just a dirty book,
splayed on the highway
makes the car swerve.

The damn ditch has the heart of a magnet.
The body of the car
can't help but abandon itself
to the slip of the ice,

in a moment of weakness.

The sinking feeling,
into three feet of snow,
was really quite brief.

But how does the tow truck
fit in?
She has to wait two hours
for it.
She doesn't even have a cigarette.

She is disgusted by this metaphor
and wants me to stop.

As she drives on,
her eyes are nailed to the road
but I make her brain slick
the furrows of the cliff.

The Adulteress in her Season

She is a new winter,
a snow burst.

Her startled hands open
all over the city
and melt a million times into the lake.

She is cast down in celebration
on roads, on pools, on slides,
on corners, caught in the greedy fingers
of every tree and bush.

Each black pencil
cries   it's light, it's light
and everything is touched.

The Adulteress and the Poem

I make her go on long walks.
I point out

the long backbone of moon
on the naked lake,

the hills that arch
beneath the sweat of snow,

the air that is the black mouth
that teaches the bone of the moon

the dark.

The Adulteress on the Beach

She can't stand
it. She feels
as if she is walking on bodies.
Her feet slip over sacks of skin
in the mattress of sand.

It's all right, I tell her,
it's a lonely art, dying even,
a real live corpse.
So lie down.
Enjoy it.
It's a cold beach.
No one reads it.
No one has to know.

The Adulteress and the Confession

Why does every word melt
into some sex thing, she asks.
Is the word a hand?
A body? What is it doing to this page?
And who is it I hear coughing?

It's only Keats.
The paper is his handkerchief.
He coughs into it.
But don't distract me with him.
I want to know
if it's good.
Does it feel wild?
Does she like it?

She says it is none of my business.
Only those sick women poets
want to absorb every soggy minute
down the slippery slope.
Paper disintegrates when it gets wet.

So . . .
it's not the poem that is coughing?
It is Keats?
The paper is his handkerchief?

She admits she likes it
when a man has a bad cough.

The Adulteress and the Communicable Disease

This month
she is living on
coffee, lust,
and ruby red cough syrup.

Over and over again,
I tell her she shouldn't dream of it.

But she licks the spoon.
She loves it,
its stickiness,
how it jolts her awake.

The Adulteress, Lunch and Masturbation

Joking aside, she didn't get any.
Everyone was too busy.
If she eats only ink
much longer
she'll look anorexic,
faint like a Gothic heroine
on every page,
her hips a rusty anchor,
thrown away.

The ink is making her sea sick,
she complains.
Her skin rolls and buckles like paper.
Is meaning sinking into the silt of words
and slowing her down?

I cannot use
her naval metaphors.
I tell her to go eat cream and bananas,
to crush some garlic in her salad.
If she can't hook her hips into a man,
she should eat alone,
milk herself for a change,
as I do.

The Adulteress and the Bear Story

When she was sixteen
her father went on a camping trip
by himself
and when he came home,
his metal cooler was scarred and bent.
He said a bear had batted it down a ravine,
bopped it like a soccer ball.
The whole family shuddered at the near escape.

Years later, she sat at the kitchen table
with her father and his new wife.
The wife said,
"Remember when that bear attacked our cooler?"

So now the bear story has grown flaws.
Rolls of teeth and fat
push against her every night,
"Oh just a little,
let me rub up against you, just a little."

I draw the sordid, sad eyes of the bear
a little better all the time,
make them fix her.

Her miserable empty blankets are not enough.
The smell of greasy fur stays on her fingers.

Who can I blame? she says,
looking in the mirror,
smelling her hands.

Memory, I say,
or, I forget, is it myth?

The Adulteress Transported
at the Dentist's

He's got her nearly upside down.
She swallows laser beams
and grains of sand.
Slivers of metal prop open her mouth.

Here the reparation is made.
She deserves a drill.
She would drink a needle.
But he merely strings another delicate hook,
dabs a little red dye.

It should hurt more,
it really should.

He's too high tech, I tell her.
But I'm slashed to the past.
I give you more —
much more —
than he does.

You are the bit
between my teeth.

The Adulteress Wants a Love Poem

Noticing that the man
seems to be as absent
as a Renaissance mistress,
she says: metaphor never
undresses a single truth.
What is this all about?
What about his heat?
His half-open eyes?
His voice damp in her ear?
The sweet whip of the bed?
His thumb? his jokes?
his caution taken up
and abandoned,
although never entirely?

I agreed this seemed unfair.
Personality is shafted.
I did remind her
of what her lover said about secrets
and rituals of cognition.

But truth!
Each poem adulterates,
so what does she expect?

The Adulteress Tries to Speak

the poem makes me do this. the poem knows more than I do.
it is the poem that wants more and more. there is nothing
more greedy than the blank page. it is a skin with a thousand
nerves. vain, it wants black touching. it wants to cram the
whole paper with itself. eat itself with its own mouth. it uses
my body. I cannot read as fast as the poem. the poem makes
itself a bed. the image is the sheet. the readers are bodies,
captive bodies because nothing can peel them off. their eyes
are wide open. words glue the bare eyes to the page. naked
they roll over the poem. that's why the poem makes me do it.
it loves the feel of open eyes sliding down its slickness. I
cannot lift the eyes off my feelings of panic. the eyeball is soft
and sticky as it moves over me. stop. close the eye. no it won't.
the images open up like lids, drip tears. the poem gets itself
drunk on   the sheets are wet   now white as the eyeball, as
glue in the classroom, as what I drink from him   the poem
gets itself down the hole of the eye   it makes me do this

I am the bed, the body, the sheets.
Open me.
Close me.
Make me.

The Adulteress' Desk is Affronted

The room swells white and sunny.
Its skin goes soft and stupid,
like volumes of Victorian verse
with their crusts of gold trim
and spongy bodies.

Outside, the snow still heaves itself down.
The sky has not moved for months,
only grown thicker,
like her library.

The paper on her desk is tedious.
No one wants it. It is research.
She coughs scraps of Whittier, Hemans.

You see, her coat, her winter coat,
is a salary she draws each morning.
The snow works its chill into her,
the spiteful paper cuts her fingers.
It comes out of her mouth,
already inked, soiled and obsolete.

Her body wants a postcard from Florida,
but I and winter use her,

stick it to her,

scholar her.

PART III

—

I WORRY ABOUT
WHAT I AM DOING

We've unbolted the gates to the foe: let's make a general
Surrender, in faithless betrayal keep our faith.
— Ovid, *The Art of Love*, Book III, 577-578

Travels in the Fall

for Jennifer G.

Some look at the fallen sunlight —
the dump of copper needles in the woods,
fat pears squatting on the orchard paths,
the dead leaves a wreck of treasure
on the lawn —

and if they're old, they go south.

For others, November is accident and cancer;
if they're ill, they disappear.
Inside the yellow tree,
a black hand gropes.
The rain fails to revive the winter grass.

We too could take the journey,
claim the road of wilted rain and gold.

We too could quest away like heroes

or instead, we could simply stop and dig,
uplift the jagged lid of road,
layer long deep holes
with electric wire, voices, water,

slowly open, slowly fill,

one dark house, one dark ditch
at a time.

Revision

There isn't a single interesting person in this village . . .
when I'm below par I'd like to blow them all up with
gunpowder.
                     — from the journals of L.M. Montgomery

Maud, Canada grafts books
on an old root in your orchard.
Some dull myth you are:
your depressed husband,
your sons who fell away,
the cramp nagging at your waist.
Why do you haunt me?

I deny you three times
in a mediocre way
on the blood red road.
You are not my mother infected
with sentiment and cystitis.
You are not. You are
not.   But I want to see
you in your handwriting.
I want to smash open the village
and cry, "Contempt is a beautiful thing!"

Come on, my smothered darling genius,
come on, now.
Hand over the gunpowder, Maud.

Known in the Community
for My Perversions

There is something piquant
about living in the land of religious-nut conservatism
when you are a sexual deviant.

Of course, it is not hard to be a sexual deviant
in such a place.
Unlike many far more admirable sexual deviants,
I hadn't planned on becoming one.
I didn't even notice when it happened.
Other people noticed first,
people I didn't even know.
When they began to write letters,
it was such a surprise!
Me! A sexual deviant!
I thought, amazed,
reading my hate mail.

It's been some time since I've been a sexual deviant.
I can't say it's anything special —
though I believe sexual deviants have more fun —
but sometimes I'd rather not be a sexual deviant,
I just want to fit in,
for there is something piquant,
something faintly *je ne sais quoi,*
cherchez la femme, un peu le French Resistance,
Pépé le Pew, vichyssoise,
mauvais anglais
perverted bitch, sexual predator, *merde-y* bastard
fundamentalist, crap-sucking awful
about living in the land of religious-nut conservatism
when you are a sexual deviant,
or even when you just want one.

Honest

I am bad. In fact,
I'm a lousy fucking liar.
You should see me in this predicament.
I can't get the shift out of my eye.
I stare in horror at the matchbooks that fall out of my purse.
I lunge for the phone, then lift it gingerly.
Certain names make me stammer.
I wear guilt like a cheap red dress.
Crusty underwear is crammed in the back of the drawer.
My eyes drop like shoes, then stockings, then skirt, then silky
                                            camisole.
If passion is a storm, I am tripping over the debris.
"What bruise?" I say,
"what scratch?"

Silly Poems by Silly Female Poets

Worms, receive a lovely feast.
Sylvia Plath at last found peace.

Poets, you and all your kind
Are the ones whom we will find
Defacing her stone, her sore, her mind.

Though worms can only mime caress
Yet penetrate her uterus,
You and all your kind are worse.

The earth will merely claim her looks.
You chew, digest and shit her books.

On the Future Occasion of the Lover Reading the Poems

In a spirit of critical inquiry
and perhaps even slightly flattered
you begin.

But soon you need a drink.
You sit beside a breeze
and toss the bad poems out.

Some so disgust you
you stuff them in your gun
and fire them into your ravine.

(mmmm, do it again:
I'd like to be canyonized.)

"Shut up. Get out of the way."
Oh, you are pissed off now.

You slam your drink down,
throw the ragged mess of handwriting
to the ground.

But the cognac
has its wee warm teeth
in you good by now —
softens you all over.
(Oh lordy, lordy she is a bitch.)
I feel the sting of a poem
here
just here at the tip of . . .

My rare lay,
bad poems are your problem,
no slight to me.

No study has ever shown a link
between great sex and great poems
and if there is one . . .

(oh who is thinking this?
these poems, these pronouns, these delicate
compliments, belong to whom?)

. . . think how many great
poets you would have known.

The Poet Envies the Musician
Her Instrument

Because it is dark and hollow inside,
yet it is made from something solid.
Because her mouth or hand must touch it.
Because she can care for it with cloth and polishes,
or else she can store it away.

Because it can be played in a semi-circle of others.
Because it can be alone and yet commanding.
Because it can be heard from behind a closed door.
Because when an artist of the Dutch school
paints it with oyster shells and a silver platter,
we call it still life, even more.

Because the music stand opens like the delicate
    bones of a fan
and the sheets of music are bolts of brocade.
Because the firelight burnishes the curves
and her lover sometimes asks her to play.

But, mostly, because it has a case.
When she carries it on the street,
everyone knows what is in it.
It contains, yet it announces,
the cushioned body of her work.

Keats and the Nectarine

September's garden unloads all shades of red:
Tomatoes, peppers, shallots, peaches, apples,
And wrists and arms leash in thick ropes of grape.
Like books, this reawakened bounty pulls
Out of us old thoughts of time, recorded
      Endlessly in odes,
           His crossed and uncrossed letters,
             Seeds and myth,
That black ploughed myth of plenty and withdrawal.
The mother's canning peaches. The glass is hot,
The core is sweet. She's storing gold below.

      The lyric bears the weight of history
      on a slender back, a thin shelf.
      Is it natural to feed on art?
      The glass jar, the earth,
      his letter of September 22, 1819,
      his nectarine?
      I do my autumn chores,
      I think of him, preserved and rarely read.
      Of schools beginning again
      and millions who will not read his poems.
      Of walls of new books,
      thee-less, thou-less,
      the best with their even shorter lives.
      Of the goddess carved open
      stupefied on a steel sheet
      as the irregular stitches
      are yanked through her skin.
      A new world is no home for his language.
      Even his letters lingered on his table
      reluctant to undertake the Atlantic crossing.
      Keats, turn back.

Turn back and look at me
as I take a knife
to the fruit's ripe and fabulous skin.

The violet veil of dusk obscures the air.
The garden's ragged, empty-handed, rope-burned.
The blackening hills turn their backs on the garden's despair.
Trapped in the stubble, the garden paces and turns.
The swallows, its anxious speech, fly up, "Oh care
            For me!" Beseeching
                    Loving words, they are
                        Scorched,
And vanish into the lengthening, opening dark.
The woman struggles to lift the brimming urn
Before the mouth is sealed and all's interred.

The Wild Doe in the Woods

Poets, step out of your rooms.
Peel yourselves, thinly,
with the blade of cool air.
Come clean.
Lay your skins down in the grass.

What? Is your skin a mountain that cannot move?
Is the air a loneliness?
How will you carry your poems?
Is your mind a vigorous wood?
Are the poems the deer?
Do their eyes startle when they feel
the stone slide from your face?

Nature has its suspicions.
Poets, poets, tell us
what you have done.

PART IV

—

THE SONNET
LESSONS

Can a Sonnet Be a Joke?

Renouncing badly timed, immoral sex
Is difficult to do. She masturbates
And cries and writes, but dreams! They still perplex
Her body, hot with touch that agitates
In that old rhetoric of skin. Can she
Enjamb another line, or chair, or limb?
Can sweet pentameter code a banshee
Wail, or moan, or just a joke for him?
Jokes are best, more fun and far less trouble,
Or so, at least, she *says* when fucking's out.
(How odd a sonnet sounds with that.) This rubble
(Nancy tweaks the beat and mucks about)
Could a finer woman build . . . Oh, stow it —
Lots of fucking makes a better poet.

How She Abandons the Renaissance Poets

I bore the hell within me, bore to tears.
The fire hardly bothers to scorch me now.
Oh, it pops a rocket or two in my brain, or jeers
As I scratch at my heart to spark an old vow,
But hell can't stick a cinder. The work is done.
This little world needs an ashy brush.
And truly, hell would like to cut and run
And find another heart to cheat and crush.
But no, poor hell must stay and make me feel
Rotten. And I swear I hurt. I *do.*
I'm burnt with pangs and stung with fire. It's real.
My skin, my lips, my cunt are hot right through . . .
      Twit. Though all torment should delight the same,
      Hell sighs and thinks: it's such a waste of shame.

But Learns Her Squash Lesson Well

Didn't dear Ovid say love, all love, is an art?
Poetic at times, one hundred and eighty degrees
Cross the compass, the two hour slide, the part
Where we hit the wall, the racket, the strokes, the rallies.
Oh, these are good rules for me! Is the quatrain the court?
And off the court, no rule's the good rule to follow?
The limerick of dressing, the golden ode of the cork,
The refrain of the bed, yes, I hear it call — oh,
I see. The afternoon is the court. The quatrain
Spills into the sonnet of hours. No rule's the rule
Outside of these lines. The art stops here. The main
Thing to remember: free verse and art's not cruel.
       It's only near athletic court, and on it,
       That you and I will ever play a sonnet.

She Thinks of Yeats in the Middle of It All

A sudden drop, the plane lands in Dublin,
Bottled in fog. The children left behind
Are still obsessed with Troy. I think of him.
Of course he thought of Leda here. Now I
Walk the broken stone in air half sea.
I think of parents, yes, of Cronos, more
Of Agamemnon. But in the *Odyssey*
The children find the world's greatest hero.
Mothers, fathers promise much, then go
And say they'll search the sodden streets — for show:
A guilty pub's their land of glass and fire.
Alone, the children form their heart's desire:
Come home. But the parents stay for others,
And weep, and drink, and lean on their new lovers.

So Does She Hate Love?

It's true that hate is a pure emotion. Yes,
Pure as lancing needle or crack of bone.
It's sweet to detonate a nerve, unless
You bungle hate with a face. So hate alone.
And lust is pure. It has just one intent:
To take a molten nail and plunge it cold.
It's sweet to suck the heat of lust if meant
To cool, but if it warms, you must withhold
Yourself for all intent's polluted then.
So lust alone. But how can lust or hate
Not have this face? You need to start again.
Purity forges a circular, singular state.
   Hate to lust and lust to hate you'll find
   Perfects the burning stake, and love's defined.

There is the Problem of the Old Recollected

It's first the sense, then memory, then words:
Words search and scratch. Why won't I let the sense
Evaporate? It's not the music heard
I still want played, not even your hands, their presence
Forever. The body's a record the poem records
For what? A museum? A theatre? A silken dress
To molest the body with fourteen strands of words
That rework touch? A skin completely senseless.
Is this desire absurd, as if I longed
To be a candy, foolish, hard and sweet —
A joke to tease, dissolve, be lost on your tongue:
The mouth to taste the words to feel the cheat?
       And if all poems melt me with this doubt,
       Your hands work best on me within, without.

If So, What Colour Are His Eyes?

My lover's eyes are nothing like the lake.
Still, I want to sail sonnets in them,
Bend little bits of paper wing and make
A tiny fleet — in fact, regatta him.
But just as boats do nothing for the lake
So sonnets can do nothing for his eyes
But form a fleeting summer picture, take
Liberties with cliché and knot the lies.
Yet the lake does something for the boats,
Allows the keels to slit its shaft of blue
Without a transformation, and only notes
The shallow, wild passions passing through.
      Without the lake, the folded boats are done.
      Without the boats, the lake still sails the sun.

Can She Play With His Metaphor?

What wayward slap is this that caught me loose?
Some wanton knot has slipped and cost the course.
Each pore of cloth is wet and wild to fuse
Its lightning white with blue. And would you force
Me right and push the wind aside to take
The charted tack? Let's take each wave ragged
And exhaust the rope. Only narrow lakes
Channel straight and never drenched or jagged.
But here you throw your weight along the line
And crack the sky with sail. Your cool eye will
Make me conform the perfect curve and mime
Control. And we'll go true and smooth until
Some other sudden shift will break the tension
And I will rip a poem from your suspension.

Sonnet 51, or She Keeps Coming Back

Fifty poems, a hundred letters and four fucks
Later — well, I've beat Dante all to hell
In sexual gratification, so I say sucks
To fame. But Nancy, darling, truth to tell
Others — say with looks or skill — do as well,
In fact, much better, without a poem or letter.
And if this sorry account cannot quell
Pathetic thrill, you are no go-getter,
Girl. Perhaps it's time to clasp the fetter
Of artful ambition, that nobler tradition
More usually vain. Sonnets can't be abettors
To artless, self-deluded manumission.
Why court the smug and lolling lovers' derision?
Go get screwed in failed *poets'* perdition.

And Going Down

Ninety kilometres an hour seems too slow
A pace to get to you — this place — tonight.
Riding the curves — I love this touch and go —
As opera makes the car a bomb, ignites
Music all over the glass, I dream your hands
Are darkness and song and this is the blinding speed
They carry me in. The brake is lost. What withstands
A taste for excess? Hurry. The road's a stampede
Leaving trampled rules, white lines behind.
Only, signs keep flashing: "Slow Down." Explosive
Voices end in silence. And then I find
I'm in the village limits, worried, submissive.
Now I stop. You meet me at the door.
Glance, just once, and then I hit the floor.

Smoking is a Major Cause of Heart Disease

And what about your office parking lot
Bare when your ink and silver car's not in it?
Surely a ten foot hole in the heart is fraught
Extreme with risk — I'll die at any minute.
Nasty habit, these metaphors. I think
Cigarettes are dear but safer. The weed'll
Ease addiction without the trip of drink,
But metaphor is junk without a needle.
Unless I write, the goddamn poem's not here.
Roads are empty except the patch you burn.
Nothing fills the beating lines with fear.
Smoking kills by inches, and, poets learn,
Metaphor by miles. The heart pumps air
Each time the gap must signify it's there.

Vita Nuova

Dante in the city — not Firenze —
Makes me rage: translation is so bland.
The words should be a bridge from sweet plain land
To tongues of air that drench the bright *canzone*.
Instead the sonnets scatter on the bay,
Each sailboat a folded, wayward page
Unknowable, unless I make the image
You and forge a bridge that carries Dante.
The heart's a bridge beating over nothing
Yet fastened to the body. The heart will leap
The salt of your mouth and dangle there, unkissed.
Only air will eat the heart; a wing
Of verse may brush your lip but not slide deep.
"Oh Christ," the aching bridge now cries, "Resist."

The argument seems clear here. Dissatisfaction with my lack
of Italian makes me think of you so I let my own language
speak and I find the dissatisfaction is in my heart and my own
words. Surely, it's time to resist all lust and strive for a new life
where renunciation leads to peace. Yes, Beatrice turned away
and would not speak. And so in English the sound of the
Italian sonnet falls into prose, briefly, for three and a half
lines, or more as when the masculine and feminine rhyme
cannot meet but with the eye. Dante, your poems lie jewelled
in their beds of prose. I understand this. It is more of the
same. But explain your future to me again. Why, oh why did it
work for you? I still can't understand the course of love, not
even when I fake Italian sonnets.

What He Knows

I hear it tear. I rip the sheets from off
The bed, all dark torn out. I hear it tear
Away. The sound is the same slow shift — so soft —
Hands make as they leave damp skin. The dark is where
The poem is sense, before the paper leaves
The pad. The pen draws out the dark beneath
The page. The pen can feel the poem through sheaves
Of cloven white. The stroke of ink is breath
That brushes hair, but always turns and moves
Away. These words must raise the paper, waste
The dark in air and eye, a tear that proves
Each pull inadequate, each draw debased.
      You know that secrets source the heart, dear one,
      And words can strip the bed, make poems withdrawn.

The Last Lesson She Has to Learn

I tidy the sonnets up for you and add
The fourteenth closing rhyme. Is the couplet a kiss
Goodbye? Two hands that fall before the sad
Blank page asserts its clean "Don't Touch"? Is this
Too sloppy for our neat arrangement? Will
I ever feel the lips of a poem close?
A door can hide a terrible mess until
It's opened. Sonnets pound until it shows.
Each time you shut your eyes and say "Enough."
But take this mess — it's yours to have and scold
Me if you think the sonnets lessen love
And don't return it wrecked but fourteenfold.
     And if it's never now until we touch,
     Tell me, truly, do I disclose too much?

PART V

—

I AM DISPOSED OF,
AS WERE OTHERS
BEFORE ME

. . . Some men have notorious reputations,
Many have ditched a mistress. Learn in time
From some other girl's cries of distress . . .

— Ovid, *The Art of Love,* Book III, 453-455

Quick Work, or an Affair Cut Short

The bed's a clock and we're the hands
That track a whole
Twelve hours in less than one.

No wonder the pin has slipped its notch
And the clock's smooth face
Has come undone.

Pain and Pleasure in the Latin Quarter

*In Paris, in the early 18th century, religious hysterics
made pilgrimages to the grave of a heretical priest buried
in the cemetery of the church of St. Médard.*

i. The Saint

I thought the wafer of granite
against my skull was my last and best communion;
but no, the earth is a stomach
and acid runs through it.
What bilious greens boil out of me.
Already the fleshy white blooms
have knocked themselves senseless
all over the graveyard and my body.
How can I pray with my body nibbled and gnawed?
Petals spoil in me everywhere,
between my ribs, staining my bones,
caught in the sockets of my eyes.
Why have I been buried facing upwards?
Why, my brothers?
Even my eternal glimpse of heaven rots.

ii. The Girl

They say that if we kneel by his stone
and eat a morsel of his dirt
from the hand of a virgin,
we will have holy visions.

We creep into the churchyard at night.
I lick my friend's fingers clean
and swoon in the black grass.

A lion steps through my body,
his claws coarse sand.
My skin is lace that sifts him.

Love of God, I roll out of the grave,
unravelled and mewing in the dewy lawn.

My skull — kiss me, dear friend —
is soft as a peeled almond
and my joints slip like pearls through my skin.

Now it's your turn.
What a delicate prickling:
your teeth and this clay
mixing so lightly in my palm.

iii. The Priest

It's foul what this rogue has become.
His grave is a brothel.
Even his stone has come loose.

Hateful virgins,
the trouble they cause.
If they must have something in their mouths,
let them choke on my black robe.

The whip in my hand is thick as a bell rope.
My lashes will be the clapper,
their white backs, the peal.

Dear God, I will teach them.

But the church is cold
and dressed in stone.
She has taken all my thought.

I look at the swollen hump of his grave,
and think:
what if happiness were a nightmare?

If so, it must be so.
Bless me, Father,
I am your servant, I pull your great tongue.
I ring the black bell of his grave
till it bleeds.

Tempests at Sea, or Troubles on Shore

wool, oysters, linen —
show me your contraband,
carve bits of ivory
out of my clothes,
sing me an ode of a curse

but while you tell tales about vessels
you have pirated
I am mocked in the surf

on the shore the cannibals
sift out of the forest

out there the storm
thumps its huge fists
on the sea

and you keep lying to me
and telling me that you are

where?

I see that you cannot restrain
your rambling designs

but is shipwreck
the best you can offer me?

SS *Abject*

Sailor, I am a sponge
on the deck of the SS *Abject*.

All day I slide around
in the emotion bucket,
in lovesick slop.

No one notices me.
Not a first mate, not even a wife.

Once in a while you pick me up,
drain a stale poem out of me,
and toss me back
where I slowly swell up again.

Ah, I am indolent and deluged.
Sloshing against the bucket walls,
I think I am safe from the cold wind

and when your hands are around my throat
I have come to call this consolation.

But today wretchedness runs through me.
Today I am loaded with what I have done.

Today you spiked the bucket with champagne
and bruised the cabin boy for fun.

In

every lake has something drowned in it
the water welded to the beach
cannot keep the bodies out

the deepest joint of the water
is infected by a worm
cold as a murderer's finger
its slow ripple the only pain
the lake ever feels

how did I get into this?

I wallow in self-pity

the truth is
I pushed my way in
I let your finger
sound me

I took you in
through every hole of my body

you even gave it to me
in the back

In the Mansion

Before anyone else, she's up early.
Except for the hundreds of whistling and squawking birds,
and someone in some other street where bells are ringing.

She sweeps the glassy floor.
And when she's done,
she looks through the wooden slats of the kitchen shutters.

Over the walled courtyard,
the bougainvillaea lifts its feather-boaed shoulders.

She is the object of a glorious shrug.

I Know, But Can't Remember, Why I Did It

All the glee the loving spills
is sucked or drunk or dried
into the sheets or mindless flesh;
the false is pacified.

But just you try to make it new,
pretend you're more than memory,
play for keeps with common life,
mock its penitentiary,

and you will never forget the day
that you are slapped in jail.
Metaphor lives to testify;
the body will always fail.

Watching the Weed Whacker in the Cemetery

She moves slowly between the rows of leaning stones.
Her workman's boots are boats
that carry her thin brown legs over the lawn.
The machine is a murderous noise
flaying the granite,
mowing down the edgy,
ducking grass.

Is she thinking,
"This is the cemetery, this is the scythe?"
Or maybe
it's just a summer job to her
and she is bitter about
how much more work there is here
than at City Hall.

The headstones are shouting their names
as she goes by
but how can she hear them?

She passes,
alive and angry in her own life

while the headstones
hang onto the graves,
their only hope.

Waste

for Holli

The climber stranded and dying on Everest
Talked to his wife in New Zealand by radio.
To be there he had thrown away all the rest
Of his life with her. On the icy slope
He was left with a last few minutes.

What could he do but describe his death
While she sat trembling in a true season
And a walled room where air and breath
Were nothing to her. Into the wire the woman
Could not press her body nor the room
Nor a few of her own so many hours.
So why did he do it, and what was it for?

She knew she'd never speak to him again.
So the shock of why it happened,
Will only be "how?" and "when?"

The Curse of Having Written Love Poems
That Mean Nothing Now

Everything the poet spills is female
and every inch of poem,
a month of life.
Don't believe it when she tells you
this is made-up.
Each four lines is equal to a curse
that pushes love and more love out
and measures
art's shameful mockery of birth.

Oh Lords of Ladies Intellectual

I chop a foot from off the beat;
To travel far he must love often.
Lord Byron, though your wit is sweet,
Your foot is severed in your coffin.
You knew that wits in women defeat
No man's limp. They merely soften.
Insult trips a balanced verse
And love could not dispose one worse.

Insomnia Afterwards

for Sue P.

there's so much misery out there
I just want to stay home
and unplug everything
but the kids track it in on the soles
of their shoes unawares
though their insouciance and clean hair
daily rinse the house inside and out
still it never ends
we have to drag shopping bags
and stupid junk and botched hearts
through doors and into our filthy cars
sawing keys back and forth over hundreds of key holes
until everyone is in bed
finally

and we join the ranks of insomniacs
who I'm sure would not be bad company if we could see them
(except for the drunk who will soon wake someone up
and smack her face)
I mean the ones who do housework at two in the morning
and then sit and have a cup of milky tea
or even those who have herbal teas
I'd even allow a small scotch
those are the ones I mean,
who listen to the washing machine
thump thump thump thump
in the basement

finding this comforting
because it sounds like some other love-lost friend
pounding her pillow over and over again
she can't sleep
she can't sleep

Peel River Bridge, Yukon Territory

Split by the icy lance of river, one strip
of road clasped by a narrow bridge goes north.
Bitter soft the tundra, naked earth.
I have made a monument: this trip
across that steel sling to a hieroglyphic
skin of moss. Nothing, nothing for the eye
but two bare palms held up towards the sky
of dying Arctic summer. Do we pick
our symbols for love, or do they just survive?
I cross the delicate, swinging bridge with him.
A drifting wolf haunts the dissolving rim.
All around, the curve of earth deprives
us of the view that offers destination.
I know, yet still can't see, the desolation.

The Two Meanings of Cleave

On the boat, he thought of an ax —
the harsh eastern ax of the Atlantic
that hacked an island off a coast.
The island crawled away from him with grief:
such fog, such weeping.
It became the shape of its wake.

In bed, she thought "unto thee."
The moon, clear and archaic as those words,
came into bed with them,
wrapped blackness round their bodies
so they were presents bound in silver ribbons, opening.

In the book, Anne of Cleves floats by on a blue wave,
blue as Renaissance paint.
In a frame of wedding dress
her skin is puffy and sallow.
Even in the wet paint
the divorce was imminent and textured.

The present embeds itself in time,
the moving blade, the sliding wedge.
Each stroke bestows another,
each act will cleave the here and gone.

Turning Loose the Swans

when the swans landed, galloping,
on the barren strip of beach beside the highway

cars swerved and almost sailed into the lake

I among them

now the birds dismantle the carriage and pack up their wings
their leathery feet cast off the traces
they pick their steps over the gravel
towards the blank lip of the water

they shift this way and that
preparing the marble gift of themselves
each feather swept and dusted

like a great museum
the lake receives them
one by one
it slowly rolls them away

I am left with stacks of paperwork
I cannot file or shelve
I juggle awkward folios over my knees
crack the spines of volumes never opened

all the while
the swans dissolve into questions
and footnotes

still, how he spoke to me!
across the lake,
a civilization,
how he made me speak

the poems became him
till there was nothing left to do
but inscribe this final page:
Ovid, dear Ovid, was my guide

ABOUT THE AUTHOR

NANCY HOLMES was born in Edmonton, Alberta and went to high school in Toronto. She received a BA and MA in English and Creative Writing from the University of Calgary where she studied poetry with Christopher Wiseman and fiction with W.P. Kinsella. In 1991, she moved to the Okanagan where she now teaches English at Okanagan University College and lives in Summerland, BC, with her husband and three teenage sons. Holmes writes both short fiction and poetry, and her work has been published in dozens of literary journals across Canada. Her first collection of poetry, *Valancy and the New World*, won the Kalamalka National Poetry Competition. Her second collection, *Down to the Golden Chersonese: Victorian Lady Travellers* (Sono Nis), consists of four poetic sequences and one short story about Victorian women who travelled the globe. She wrote the poems in *The Adultery Poems* over the past eight years, revising and rewriting when she could, while juggling a full time job and raising kids.

MEMBER OF SCABRINI MEDIA

Quebec, Canada
2002